THE
TRUE SOLUTION

OF

The Present Religious Difficulties

- AS SHOWN IN

AN ADDRESS

TO HIS HOLINESS

POPE PIUS IX., AND THE PÈRE HYACINTHE.

With an Appendix,

AND A LETTER FROM THE

HON. W. E. GLADSTONE

AND OTHERS.

BY

MRS. LAIRD, OF STRATHMARTINE.

LONDON:
E. WESTERTON, 27 ST. GEORGE'S PLACE, S.W.
1875.

THE

TRUE SOLUTION

OF

The Present Religious Difficulties

AS SHOWN IN

AN ADDRESS

TO HIS HOLINESS

POPE PIUS IX., AND THE PÈRE HYACINTHE.

With an Appendix,

AND A LETTER FROM THE

HON. W. E. GLADSTONE

AND OTHERS.

BY

MRS. LAIRD, OF STRATHMARTINE.

LONDON:
F. WESTERTON, 27 ST. GEORGE'S PLACE S.W.
1875.

LONDON:
JOHN STRANGEWAYS. Printer, Castle Street, Leicester Square.

THE TRUE SOLUTION

OF THE

PRESENT RELIGIOUS DIFFICULTIES.

———◆———
.

An Address to the Rev. Père Hyacinthe, by
an English Lady :—

GENEVA,
17th of October, 1873.

REVEREND PÈRE HYACINTHE,—

It gives me great pleasure to meet you and
make your acquaintance, for although I am only a
woman, I have thought deeply over the religious
difficulties of the present day ; and like many others,
who are earnest, I have wished to see all matters
connected with religion in a more perfect practical
state upon earth.

I am happy to behold, in you, one of the chief
pioneers towards that perfectibility so difficult for
human nature to attain unto. Throughout all ages
the Christian world has been torn and rent by opposite extremes, the worst of human passions have been
enkindled in mistaken zeal for the religious cause
and those, who would have been the best friends of

their God and Redeemer, have, alas! been His greater enemies. And is it not so still? I ask, therefore, can nothing be done in this wonderful age of progress and improvement to change the mistakes of man in the all-important subject of his religion? Difficult as such measures have ever been found by the wise and good men of the past, and may still be found by those of the present, yet hopefully would I say that, with God's help, a more perfect union of Christians and Christian life may yet be achieved. Have the means used in the past always been the right and best means? Cannot gentle persuasion, a consistent course of action, and a pure system based upon the simple truth of God's will, induce men to worship Him out of a feeling of *love alone?* Cannot they be taught that it is a *privilege*, given to mortal being, to bow down and worship the Creator of us all? And cannot man find his happiness in such an act? I believe that many more would do so if they had the truth and the practice of the truth placed before them in one uniform system, in which the ignorant and even more enlightened class of mankind would not be repulsed, as they too often are, by the deformity of the preaching and teaching they receive. If public worship could be made uniform and legitimately attractive by the adoption of the happy medium between extremes; if the priest or minister would preach the truth earnestly, lovingly, and firmly,— would not all classes of mankind show a willingness instead of a reluctance to appear before Almighty God? And thus, with the aid of His Sacraments and His Holy Spirit, they would learn to battle with evil, and drive it from their hearts by the resolute exercise of the all-powerful love of goodness, with its beneficent attributes; they would not only thank God for His mercies 'with their lips, but with their lives.' What is chiefly required in these days is *help to make men honest*—honest in religion, honest in his relation to his fellow-man. To be AFRAID to *injure* each other, as being one of the worst and most deadly sins he can commit; because, as the Scripture saith, 'If we love not our brother whom we have seen, how can we love Him whom we have not seen?' We need more JUSTICE in the world, to do to others as we would others should do to us; these should not be *mere words*, but should be religiously acted upon. In every class more love of truth, more justice, is terribly needed, whether amongst the highest in social position, or in the courts of law, in other professions, in trade or miscellaneous employments, or in the social relations of life. Let men be taught that it is WORTH WHILE (even from so low a ground) to be good and upright; to have a clear conscience both towards God and his neighbour; to act both in spiritual and temporal affairs from the *highest principles*, no matter what amount of suffering it may cost him; to suffer himself to be pinned to the cross if necessary, rather than *shirk* the moral courage required to force himself to do what is right; and also let him feel that if at any moment he fail, through human infirmity, and he is unhappy and sorry for his fault, he has but to confess it to a loving Father, who for His dear Son's sake will instantly pour down His full and perfect forgiveness; let the penitent on no account go to *man* for ABSOLUTION, for our Creator alone is *Judge;* let him rather rise up from his knees—from his painful visit to the Throne of Grace, clothed in *manly courage,* without fear of man; let him start afresh on the right path, and as he has picked himself up this time, so may he watch and pray against another fall, as any additional stumble will make his soul more sad. The simple lesson of right and wrong should from the earliest age be emphatically instilled into children, and although there will always remain the existence of evil in this imperfect world, which is an apprenticeship or training for another, yet by the use of God's appointed means for the improvement and salvation of His children, in due time, the scale of excellence may considerably outweigh the scale of evil. Surely careful distinction should be made by man, when judging of another, between a fall arising from *infirmity,* and one made by *wilful sin;* the first should be softened by human *sympathy,* the latter punished by a strong disapprobation *until repentance* showeth itself; when the one sinned against should at once and for *ever* blot out the fault of the sinner with the utmost charity; for except in cases of *wilful sin,* man has no right to interfere with his fellow-man. To preserve his self-respect and true dignity, every soul should endeavour to stand *alone* with his Creator, to go continually to His dear Son, and speak with Him of himself, as to the dearest friend through time and eternity, and to whom alone he belongs, or upon whom he has just claim, through the strength of his Redeemer's promise, saying, 'He who cometh unto *Me* I will in no wise cast out.'

I have lately been shocked to see the disrespect unscrupulously shown in the cause of right *versus* wrong in human matters, that is, where it is more to the worldly interest of an individual to support wrong-doing or false principle. The weak and unprotected are too often oppressed by those who are rich and powerful, who readily find willing tools and sup-porters in their inhuman work of persecution. Of course it has been so in all ages, man's inhumanity to man is proverbial; but when, in these enlightened days, a man of position and a member of the medical profession, boldly asserts, as I have heard him assert (and with no air of sorrow for the assertion) that right principle never answers,' *ergo*, it is folly to exercise it; and also adds—'the world will never be better,' that if an individual is oppressed and per-secuted by enemies, and has but few friends to sup-port him in the day of need, he ought not to expect to meet with common justice; and further, when this gentleman objects to hear the sacred name of God repeated in conversation, although uttered with the deepest reverence, as the voice of authority, when no doubt he is accustomed to hear the Almighty's name taken in vain amongst men in society without giving a reproof that it is sinful so to do,—what, indeed, can be expected in the way of the world's improvement, if such sentiments become general? Again, this same person, in an interview with a stranger whom he knew had long borne patiently a painful misrepresentation, repeated this, and more, in his adherence to might against right. The stranger turned, like a worm that is trodden under foot, and proudly spoke the indignation which such false sentiments called forth; upon which, the medical professor and interested man of the world ingeniously changes the provoked warmth of feeling into a personal affront, and affectedly leaves the room, demanding the charity of which he himself is so totally devoid. What can one do but cry *shame* upon such an one, and in wishing him to repent, hope that he may henceforth uphold virtue at any price, and in however small a degree to endeavour to lessen the lump of iniquity which abounds. In alluding to this particular case, which has been brought before my notice, I wish to illustrate how much more than I could have believed a false principle is fostered in society, and how *little trouble* is taken to follow what is true and right, where it is considered better worth while to side with the strongest party; a laxity of principle is even laughed at—treated lightly as though it were a joke.

And now, dear Sir, I am going to speak of Roman Catholicism; and as an Englishwoman, a member of the National Church, I speak without prejudice or ill-feeling towards the Romish Church or the Vatican. On the contrary, I have the greatest respect for the Church of my forefathers, to which, in one sense, I consider both you and I,—and, indeed, all Christians —still belong. *We* have not changed our faith; the erroneous changes have arisen with the Popes, and their coadjutors: *we* are for ever members of the Holy Catholic and Apostolic Church, and we inherit the same truth as was taught in the Primitive Church of Christ. I ask you, is it not so, dear Sir? We hold the same doctrines, the same practice that Christ

9

Himself taught when upon earth: the opposition and disapproval exhibited by the so-called Protestants is simply shown towards the *human element* in the Romish Church,—human arrogance, exacting compulsory obedience from man, and to the errors which have grown up from age to age. They may at first have arisen from mistaken views; for, by degrees, man can make himself believe much that is erroneous and false, especially when he is under undue influence exercised upon the point upon which he is most sensitive,—affecting, as it is declared, his happiness in this world and the salvation of his soul in eternity; or it may be that, when the Popes have looked down from the pinnacle of the Vatican upon rebellious man, it may have been deemed *necessary* to *compel* the human soul to come to its Saviour, and so by any means, legitimate or not, to rule with a rod of iron rather than man should lose his salvation. I repeat, then, in the first instance, the intention may have been excellent; but, in their zeal, the Popes and priests have been carried away beyond what Almighty God has required of them; and, although they may have obtained many followers through this human influence, as well as through fear, the agency used has been contrary to God's law,—which has been exceeded. The result has been that many people have been driven into hypocrisy, or made poor, servile, unhappy creatures, who, as yet, know not the truth as it is in Jesus,—who are unable to enjoy the innocent pleasures and beauties of this world because they have been, by their imposed submission, deprived of the glorious liberty of the sons of God. The

Christian Gospel is the Gospel of persuasion, and the acceptance of it is voluntary, not compulsory. Christ graciously asks us to *love Him* above all created things, to take Him into our hearts, and to renew this reception from time to time by receiving His blessed Sacrament, ordained for man's benefit and comfort. The frequent renewal of this Sacrament, taken in faith, keeps the soul healthy, helps it to eschew evil, and quickens it to everlasting life. Christ expects us also to *suffer* with Him if called upon to do so; yet not to take *unnecessary* suffering upon ourselves, but, under any circumstances, to stand by Him through this troublesome life, when hereafter He will, of His goodness, bestow upon us the reward of a heavenly crown, with heavenly rest and bliss. In order to satisfy myself, I have looked into the Catholic religion,—have prayed in their churches, have spoken to a few priests, and demanded an explanation of their devotions and doctrines, which, until they are closely investigated, are altogether mysterious and unintelligible to an ultra, or even ordinary, Protestant; and from the ignorance of the latter anent the practical part of Catholicism much injustice has arisen towards Catholics and their system. We all do sin in going to extremes. In order to find *Truth*, we must take the pains to discriminate between the subtle distinctions dividing and balancing the true from the false. That is what I have endeavoured to do. At one time the Church of Rome had great attractions for me, endowed as I am with a hearty love of devotion, the appreciation of the beautiful in religion so exalting to the soul, elevating it above the

common cares or materialism of our existence. I was
on the point of joining in membership this attractive
Church. In my day of sorrow and suffering the
celestial style of worship soothed me; and I sincerely
assert that through this channel,—of being able to
enter a church alone, and, unnoticed, to go and kneel
before an altar made sacred by the Spiritual Presence
of our blessed Lord,—I have been brought nearer to
Him,—have realized His Divine Presence most perfectly within my soul; and this is what I never arrived
at in our more cold and unattractive mode of worship.

After my return from a long sojourn in India, I
found my parish church changed in form of worship;
it had adopted these accessories we now see developed
into Ritualism, and which grow and increase, albeit
the innovations are found so obnoxious to the party
called Evangelical. I was readily pleased with the
warmer devotion in the church, and thought we had
arrived at the desired improvement in public worship,
notwithstanding these improvements were borrowed
from Rome; but, after a time, I was yet unsatisfied,
for the priests and leaders of Ritualism became dic-
tatorial—they exacted *private confession*, with other
objectionable elements of Rome, until at last they
have 'out-Heroded Herod'—and that too, without
the approval or sanction of the Pope, who smiles, and
thinks the 'Anglicans' are leading their congregations
to him! I was then brought to question myself, and
consider whether it would not be better to go to
Rome at once—for, undoubtedly, *Ritualism*, with all
its life and heartiness, has failed to be a *pure middle
path*. And, as it happens, I shall never regret that

through this failure I was led to the Romish Church; for I am indebted to that Church for much valuable information, with an enlargement of spiritual experience—for much consolation in attending their altars at a time of trial and isolation, which, but for this comfort, might have been unendurable. And, as in similar cases, the mind in contending with uncontrollable emotions might have given way,—and, as if I had been nailed to the Cross—I now found Jesus there, and more intimately than I had known Him before. Man could not comfort me, and yet throughout my trial there was an affectionate friend who urged me to become a member of the one true Church. I might have been received into its membership by one of the most popular priests in England, many good souls were praying for me; but, just as I was giving myself up, the true dignity of human nature revolted at the thought of having to confess to a *man*, as well as to give assent to the declaration required by the Church, to serve it blindly in all matters, as well as to render undue worship to the Blessed Virgin. It suddenly seemed as if an overpowering rush of Invisible Spirits surrounded me to prevent me taking a step to which my conscience did not honestly respond. I accepted the warning, and as suddenly told my kind friends I must abandon my wish to enrol myself a member of their corporation. I am sorry to say their conduct changed a little towards me upon hearing my final and firm decision. This change, which was more than mere disappointment warranted, proved to me there was a FLAW in the Romish system. It was as though each one who tried to influence me was entitled to a higher heavenly place in reward for his share in introducing me to his Church I have often said to my Catholic friend, 'If I enter your Church, I shall not be a greater Christian than I now *desire* to be. I am not a *Heathen*, perfectly ignorant of the blessed Bible and its truths.' And I must confess the idea of being *re*baptized, and treated like a Heathen, rather *nettled* me. Thus, since the above given episode in my religious experience, I have remained a communicant in my own English National Church, and my acquaintance with Rome has endued me with greater charity towards all denominations of Christians. I equally, however, abjure either extreme, whether of Ultramontanism or of Ultra-Protestantism; both are equally uncharitable, though, perhaps, they don't mean to be so. Both parties lose the essence of Christianity by their intolerance and tyranny. The numerous and increasing divisions amongst Christians are deeply to be regretted. There is much *talk* about religion in the present day, and it is natural that the human heart should desire to learn the road to Heaven, since each one desires to arrive there at last. A great conflict is going on in the religious world. I am told on all sides that bishops, priests, and the laity of every nation desire a reunion of Christendom; but so difficult is it for all men to agree as to the means of accomplishing the scheme, that it is supposed to be quite impracticable --a chimera which is never to be realised till Christ Himself appears again upon earth to purify it; to show mankind how wilfully blind they are; how each one loves himself better than his Lord, and so shall

we all stand before Him *humiliated* for our pettiness
of thought, feeling, and action. We shall stand
abashed in the *Real Presence* of One who is *all
humility*, though He be the King of Kings and the
Lord of Lords.

I believe a universal practical uniformity of public
worship to be the true solution of the difficulty, which
has hitherto existed, for the nearer accomplishment of
the *union of Christendom*. The Catholic and Primitive
Church enjoyed this uniformity, and why should we
not all with one consent return to it as our heritage
and right? In consideration of our Lord's great love
to us, cannot we Protestants put aside some educational prejudices, some self-love, some self-sufficiency,
and try to accomplish that which will bring a
blessing to all mankind? Let both extremes make
use of the *compensating balance*—the compass to steer
us between the Scylla and Charybdis, which threaten
to pitch us into a useless, unprofitable, stormy conflict,
where there will be no peace, no rest. Our lives are
passing from us daily. Why not work together for
good in this generation, and thereby leave a goodly
heritage to the generation to come? As a divine
finger emerging from the cloud of difficulty, as a still
small voice from above, I behold and hear a beginning
to the desired union in the particular course of action
adopted by you, Père Hyacinthe, in the honest renun-
ciation of the errors of Rome, on the one hand, with
the firm adherence to the preaching, doctrine, and
mode of worship of our *Primitive* Catholic Apostolic
Church, on the other; or, as your adherents must
have a name amongst men, let them be called

'Liberal Catholics'— the true reformers of the Romish Church; and in this form we will be prouder still of the *divine* name of *Christian*.

I cannot presume to speak of Church government. It is for you and wiser heads than mine to organize the most practical and perfect system for the future, since you are now cast off by the Vatican. My fullest sympathy is yours; for who like yourself can form an idea of the bitter trial it has cost you to break with the old and most cherished associations in the past? But you have acted *nobly* and for conscience sake, and you are *right*. May God's Holy Spirit be with you to guide your noble mind and spirit through the many difficulties connected with the great work which is set before you. You are not guilty of *schism*, as your opponents would have us believe; and I venture to assert that in due time the thorny path of obstruction will be cleared, if only as *Christians* we work together; if each individual would stedfastly refuse an assent to the false chains of Rome; if each Protestant would cease to think his belief and practice full and perfect by unhesitatingly casting away his prejudices; and if every denomination would worship according to the Catholic Faith, as now practised by you, dear Sir, they would prove the union of Christians, in following the most perfect form of worship upon earth—the most acceptable to Almighty God; for, undoubtedly the celebration of mass is the truest idea of Christian spiritual worship. It is the commemoration of the One Perfect Sacrifice already made by our Lord of Himself. The breaking of bread in the Sacrament— the taking of Christ spiritually within ourselves through the outward means appointed, even in the form of a *wafer*—ought to be sufficient to satisfy any Christian mind ; for after this manner there is nothing contrary to God's will. Let not Protestants in Great Britain fear to worship after the form of their forefathers in the celebration of the mass, or cavil about small matters which, if better understood in the use, are found to be beneficial, and not altogether without meaning. We are not told to believe in transubstantiation,—this belief being an innovation since the foundation of the Christian Church. We are simply to believe that the act of consecration of the elements by the officiating priest brings down from Heaven a renewal of spiritual essence, which will nourish our souls to everlasting life. Let us no longer fear to look up to a beautiful, well-decorated altar, raised in our Redeemer's Name and to his honour. It is intended to *remind* you of what is *beyond*, and suggests to all, Come and adore Christ ; do homage to His Spiritual Presence ; and then the act of faith shown forth in public worship will be a real comfort to your souls. The mass may be said in the language of the country, if preferred, and suitable prayers added at will. And why should not our hearts and eyes be lifted up to the lights and symbols of the altar,—our Saviour's portrait placed there, midst flowers, and candles, to symbolize the Light of the World ? Why not have angelic music—the priest robed in a rich and suitable garment, without the *over parade* of it, as seen in Ritualism ?—Incense, too, to honour Jesus, as the wise men of old honoured Him ? We should not fear to use material substances as an outward means of grace,—or even of making the sign of the Cross, for there is great comfort in its right use,—and as an outward confirmation of what we realize within the heart. Let us also bow the head and knee at the mention of the name of Jesus,—not doing it as in the sight of men, but to show our reverence to the God who made us and redeemed us. Again, be not afraid to honour, without giving Divine or undue worship to, the blessed Virgin, the mother of our Lord, who for Christ, her dear Son's sake, is worthy to be honoured, and oftener remembered with the deepest regard. It is written, ' She shall be called " Blessed " by all generations.' We do well, therefore, to remember her in our prayers, together with the apostles, martyrs, and saints who are gone before. The dear departed of our own kindred should also be remembered and blessed. Such rules for Divine worship will be approved of by Almighty God, for such is a reasonable and right service,—avoiding coldness, on the one hand, and an approach to Pagan idolatry, on the other. In Germany, the Liberal Catholic movement is gaining favour. May it increase and prosper, and *true Reform* be maintained in its integrity, avoiding the destruction of every beneficial part of Catholicism. I regret to hear the Jesuits have been expelled from Germany, because it is using the un-Christian weapon of persecution so skilfully handled by the Jesuits themselves. Why should the Jesuits or the good old Pope be feared ?—both of whom, with the dogma of infallibility, would soon cease to exist, or become harmless, if Christians as a

B

body, under the name of Liberal Catholics, would firmly combine their unity under one banner.

I am visiting this part of the continent of Europe for the first time, and I am startled with the inconsistency of the so-called Protestants. They who have broken away from Rome, have mercilessly torn down the beauteous helps to religion which might be legitimately used to exalt the soul of mortal being—for it must be borne in mind that we are but mortal yet, and cannot realize the *Invisible* without the outward auxiliaries alluded to. The churches in Switzerland, built originally for the purpose of Divine worship, with rich architectural beauties, now dismantled, look like cold vaults, without life or spirit. I am told that even the preaching has sunk into mere Rationalism. And, worse than all, they retain the heathen practice of violating the day of rest, appointed by God for man's own benefit. How sad to see no reverence paid to our Sunday, or thankfulness for its privileges! And yet these people call themselves Protestants! Surely they will reform such an un-Protestant mistake, and learn to enjoy the day of rest without desecration ; avoiding also the mistake made in Scotland and other Protestant countries of turning the Sunday into a day of gloom and heaviness. If we love the Author of all Good, we should rejoice in the *sober liberty* which makes us free. If our churches are made sufficiently attractive, and compatible with truth, we shall on this day hasten with loving hearts to the Throne of Grace, to stand together, and yet each soul ALONE *with its Maker.* There to ask, first, forgiveness of

our sins, to pray for all who are dear, and, above all
to 'praise the Lord for His goodness to the children
of men;' afterwards to hear the appointed priest
preach the blessed truths contained in the Scriptures,
and which cannot be too often repeated. Hitherto,
when men have wished to reform the religious system,
they have *deformed* it. It remains for the leaders of
Liberal Catholicism to preserve a more perfect practice
than has hitherto been attempted by others. I
reiterate that, too often, the worship of God degene-
rates into no worship, and the preaching becomes
lowered to what is called Rationalism and Unitarian-
ism; and when one beholds this most lamentable of
all mistakes, one is almost inclined to agree with
Archbishop Manning, when he says, 'The fear exists
that when one part of the Catholic belief is pulled
down, the whole of it may fall, and even end in the
disbelief of the Incarnation of the Son of God. Alas!
it is frequently the case that Rationalism takes the
place of Christianity; but 'tis no reason that the
wheat should not be separated from the tares, and the
husbandman boldly strike his scythe for the preservation of the perfect middle path of beauty, cutting
down the weeds on either side which at present
obstruct the growth of the flourishing crop, which is
growing up in clearness and readiness for the coming
day of the General Harvest. We are not called upon
to accept falsehood in our desire to retain the truth,
nor may we give up a good portion of the truth, and
so sink into feebleness. Perhaps the very means the
Ultramontanes adopt for the preservation of truth,
defeats its object; for by exacting so much that is

puerile in worship, they leave the reasonable man no alternative than to degenerate into Rationalism—or an intellectual worship of the Creator. I hear that Frenchmen, as a rule, have little or no religion. May their fault not emanate from this very cause? They are asked to give themselves up to a belief in an *outer growth*, which belongs not to the simple truth of the Gospel, and they turn from both, in despair. Let them try Liberal Catholicism, and a Frenchman's good qualities may yet be increased and purified. It may even lead him to greater stability in *politics* and all else that is good. But, in speaking of *politics*, I would have it well understood that on no account should they be incorporated with religion; for what considerable mischief has already arisen from this undesirable union! Liberal Catholics have, happily, abolished private confession—one of the most *pernicious* of human inventions, spoiling the dignity of human nature. Nothing material should come between the soul and its Maker. *Christ alone!* is the text of the Liberal Catholic. Undoubtedly the appointed priest or minister should be honoured in his high office, and we should be thankful for the help he may be to us: and if they are but human, like ourselves, if all are not equally gifted, let us not too readily murmur, but pray that the preacher may at least be EARNEST in his preaching, for such it is his bounden duty to strive to become. Another point for consideration. Instead of closed convents, let us encourage the same kind of institution without secresy or vows, that good women, without particular home duties, may serve their God and needy fellow creatures, under a well-organised community with a suitably chosen head to it.

After some such manner, is it not possible for us all to be *one*? Surely we shall be doing right if we individually and collectively strive for this desired unity. And, if it be ever attained, the one God and Father, the one Son our Redeemer, with the one Holy Spirit which we all invoke, would, with the company of angels above, look down with approval upon mankind upon earth. And if my poor, weak words can induce and persuade any of my dear fellow-Christians to unite with the Liberal Catholics, I shall be grateful to Almighty God in that *He* has moved me to speak; I shall rejoice and say, 'All glory be to Thee, Holy, Holy, Holy, Lord God Almighty, who wast, and art, and art to come.' I speak from the heart when I repeat my desire for the union of Christendom, as in *India* I have with pain noticed how great an *impediment* to the progress of Christianity are the *divisions* among Christians. I have heard an intelligent native gentleman remark, 'Why do you English try to make us Christians? You are no better than we; nor can you agree in what you teach. One missionary tells us one thing, another the direct opposite; what are we to believe? You teach so many religions.' The natives generally prefer the Romish teaching, as there is a particle of Paganism in its forms and processions, and it teaches but ONE THING. Our religion should also be as *disinterested* as possible; and there should be no difficulty or shortcomings on the part of the laity in liberally supporting their clergy, who are entitled to a moderate and sufficient allowance for their duties in office. As I have already stated, *the Mass* and Benediction Services are preferable to the ' Dearly beloved brethren ' of the English Church, or either the Dissenting or the Scotch practice of depending upon the ability of the one minister officiating. But I must leave the further development of these cursory remarks to wiser and more experienced heads. I am but an honest Englishwoman, loving truth and straightforwardness, as one who has suffered for the truth's sake. I must not, however, omit to add that in *private devotion* we should read and study the *Holy Scriptures ;* prayers should be uttered from the heart to God,— for, remember, that no amount of devotion to the SAVIOUR can be EXCESSIVE. It is, therefore, to be encouraged by *every help.* Sacred pictures and private altars are perfectly *legitimate,* and may rouse the soul to soar above ; the private altar, with Christ's Spiritual Presence, may become a daily, personal friend in sorrow or in joy.

And now, in conclusion, I would have it clearly understood that I have no wish to start a *new religion,* nor to worship the good Père Hyacinthe as the leader of Reform. The religion which he advocates is the *primitive Catholic faith ;* and you, dear Sir, I honour as the supporter of this old faith.

Adieu, Père Hyacinthe. With you I wait and hope for better days in the Christian world,—that the Grand Union may be accomplishsd throughout all nations and all lands.

P.S.—Since writing the above, I have had the happiness of hearing a service, together with a remarkable address given by you, dear Sir, on Sunday, October 19th ; and both the service and the address were what I might have expected from you. My heart and mind responded in perfect harmony with all I saw and heard. I found there the perfect *middle path* which I have so earnestly hoped to find, and I am now happy and hopeful for the future of Christ's Church upon earth. May I beg you to receive my congratulations upon your recent election as curate of Geneva, as well as upon the more recent happy domestic event in **your** home circle.

I remain, dear Sir,

Yours in Christ,

AN ENGLISHWOMAN.

Letters of approval from the Right Hon. W. E. Gladstone, Père Hyacinthe, and a Russian Lady:—

HAWARDEN CASTLE, CHESTER,
October 22nd, 1874.

DEAR MADAM,—

I have read with interest your Address to Père Hyacinthe of October 7th, which has followed me here. Should you be pleased to forward to me the documents you name, I shall not fail carefully to peruse them. At the same time my occupations are such, and so much in arrear, that I am uncertain whether it will be in my power to offer any comment on them. I would suggest for your consideration whether you could send copies of them to the Right Rev. Dr. Von Döllinger, Munich; H. Vander Tann Strausse, and the Right Rev. Bishop Reinkens, Bonn.

I have the honour to remain,

Dear Madam,

Your very faithful Servant,

W. E. GLADSTONE.

TRAINENT, PRES GENÈVE,
24th December, 1873.

DEAR MADAM,—

Your published letter to Père Hyacinthe is entirely appreciated by him, not only on account of the noble Christian spirit that prompted it, but for its merits—its truths.

In Christo,

EMILIE J. LOYSON.

Madame Laird.

MADAME,—

La lecture de votre brochure m'a causé un vrai plaisir, et j'y ai trouvé des idées qui me peut tout à fait sympathiques. Je l'ai lû aujourd'hui et ne sachant pas si j'aurai le plaisir de vous rencontrer encore à Genève, je me hâte de vous dire combien j'ai été charmée de cette lecture. Si vous veuliez avoir l'amabilité de m'envoyer votre carte, Madame, je vous en serai pert reconnaissante, et c'est dans l'esperance de connaître votre nom, que je vous prier de recevoir l'expression de mes sentiments de parfaite considération et estime.

BARONNE SOPHIE MELLER ZAKOMELSKI.

Le Dimanche $\frac{1}{15}$ Septembre.

IT was not originally my intention to publish or
make known my address to His Holiness the Pope,
because my vision in sleep seemed too sacred an
event for publication, but my scruples have since
been overruled, and I now believe it to be the will
of Heaven that these sacred facts should be promulgated. I may here state that I have had the
honour of being presented to His Holiness.

Why Protestants in England are afraid of the
word denoting the primitive form of Christian public
worship, called the Mass, can only be understood in
the fatal term *prejudice*, comprising as it does in-
tuitive mistake of its meaning. Protestants should
pause and consider how at the time of the Reforma-
tion their new school of theology took fright at the
errors which had crept into the Christian Church by
men who exceeded their Divine power; that, instead
of calmly reorganising the system, they in rough excitement cast down every doctrine and every beauty
of the temporal spiritual Church, as instituted by
Christ Himself; and that at this particular moment
Christ shows his Protestant servants that, however
well-intentioned their motives may have been, they too
have erred in destroying His own self-appointed means
of grace. The Ritualists in the Church of England
have tried to restore the old form of worship, but, as
it is a novelty from its long disuse, it has not been

favourably received, or, perhaps, correctly introduced by them. They also have failed in restoring what Christ is now showing us He wishes to be restored; and He would have us understand that the true and only way in which His commands can be obeyed according to His will is in the reform of the Roman Catholic Church. When this takes place, Protestants must meet the Pope halfway, and again take up in its true form what for three generations has been abolished. Dr. Döllinger, Père Hyacinthe, and others have the true ideas of Christianity, and, sooner or later, their views, which are Christ's views, will be promulgated. Every religion has had the form of a sacrifice; and there is no religion without it. The sacrifice of the Mass is no fresh sacrifice; it is simply built upon the One Great Sacrifice once and for ever made for us. But what we have to understand is that Christ instituted His Sacramental Supper of bread and wine to be perpetually offered up in memorial of His death; and without this sacrifice our Christian religion is dead, and becomes a poor, meaningless thing—a vague, hazy belief in our adorable Saviour—instead of a soul-comforting reality. Christ has permitted Protestantism to exist for three hundred years, and He would now have both extremes meet in the restoration of the true form of Christianity, whereby each soul may be nourished to everlasting life, that through partaking in His propitiation of our sins we may join our sacrifice with His own. What terrible mistakes are made by extreme parties, yet it is only through them we can perceive and learn the just middle way; for example,

I remember thinking the same with regard to the Government changes, which took place at the time of the Indian Mutiny. Instead of reorganising the Native Army upon a surer basis, they almost abolished it, and sent out double the number of English troops to India. Considering the unhealthy climate, would it not have been better to have increased the English army more moderately, and kept up the full number of native troops upon a different footing? It would have been less expensive to our Government, and more advantageous to our country, and especially to India. But with regard to our *Christian faith*, it is of far greater importance that we should blend the two extremes. The Church of England should be reorganised to meet the other Episcopalian churches, and a calm moderation should be carried out in all things. Let us face the difficulties; let us sink self-interest with Protestant prejudice, in order to restore the primitive Christian religion, as Christ intends it to be restored. The violent prejudices of the many sects will not be easily allayed; they are too obstinate to understand that they or their forefathers could possibly have made a mistake. Some of the clergy, more convinced, should take the lead, and lead gently on; for the rest, they must be left alone until they feel disposed to come home and leave their mistakes behind them. As to the State question, it seems to me that the government of each nation should independently and as a Divine duty make an allowance to the support of the Church and clergy; and every person of the laity should contribute conscientiously according to his worldly means, feeling it a paramount **duty to give** *first* **to** God's ministers as giving to Him. The head of the Universal Church, with his bishops of each nation, should alone govern Church matters. Time will not permit me to give more than the skeleton of a system, the forming of which requires all the ability of our many gifted men in the Church. Our beloved and gracious Queen, of whom as an Englishwoman I am most proud, and for whom I feel a profound affection, is at this moment placed in a difficulty in her position as the temporal head of the English Church, seeing how at this moment its members are divided. I have no doubt, if the majority of her subjects desired it, she would gladly resign her authority of the temporal headship to a Divinely-appointed pope or archbishop, providing the said pope would rule by *moral force*, as was originally intended. May we soon see the happy change of a universally constituted Christian Union!

To His Holiness Pope Pius IX. and his Colleagues in Council.

MONSIEUR et MESSIEURS,—

With all due respect for your exalted position,
I, an Englishwoman, venture to approach your foot-
stool, with the one earnest object of pleading before
you, in behalf of the temporal and spiritual welfare
of the whole human race. May it please you to
listen for a moment to the small, but I believe
divinely inspired voice, who, in thus asking to be
heard, feels it is not itself who speaks ; but the voice of
Heaven through it. Human infirmity may make my
efforts of expression imperfect, but, nevertheless, with
complete disinterestedness, I desire to see the will of
God accomplished, and the greater happiness of mankind upon earth established. For the past two years
an immovable, and almost involuntary earnestness
has taken possession of my heart and mind ; it is as
though God had given me a great work to do : and,
with His Divine assistance, I will at least give utter-
ance to my thoughts, and leave the Almighty to
accomplish the rest by bestowing upon you a listen-
ing ear. We see in the present day that great
changes have come over the earth ; with the increase
of population, and the ingenuity of man, many fresh

outlets have been opened for the development of man's mind, and his natural power of acquirement—he is rapidly progressing to the highest state of development obtainable,—and, although there is a *limit* to the progress, man will, through the school of science, and by other means, attain unto that height, and that limit. We may regret much that we see in the way of abuse, in the exercise of man's cleverness, and power,—but we need not *fear* it, when we remember that it is the Divine Head that is working amongst mankind, the strings of this world's machinery are cords moved by a power stronger than mortal strength created by the Almighty, for His own Divine purpose —His children may sometimes stumble, and rebel, but God will check them, or give them liberty as He deems best, in order to accomplish the *end* He has in view. So let the natural world live on—let every man try to teach himself, and one the other—let conflict arise, and the peacemakers subdue the conflict ; let the battle of life rage, and be succeeded by peace and rest,—for so it must be in the present state of existence, but a time is approaching when order will be brought out of chaos, by the Supreme Power who is working all things together for good for those that love Christ—mark well, 'for those who love Him,'—for the rest, who do not, there will be great misery, great unhappiness. As in the world's work, so is it in the *present* day with God's spiritual and supernatural work. The time has arrived for a change towards greater perfection ; and it is as clear as noonday to me, that God wills the Roman Catholic Church from the Head, throughout every member of its body.

to effect this change, this reform, without altering its first principles, which are unchangeable; the reform from the errors of man may be made *peaceably* for all parties—if some will not be obstinately blind to the authority of their Master—and if they refuse to see the appointed way, then the great work will be accomplished through conflict, agitation, and unhappiness. To avoid such a catastrophe, let me entreat your Holiness to listen, and perform the gigantic duty assigned you ; be perfectly *disinterested*, and show the world at large, that you are capable of sinking every thought of *self* in your aspiration for the general welfare of the Christian world.

Were I the Head of the Universal Church upon earth, I would with becoming dignity stand up and proclaim before all the world,—Men and Brethren, we, the successors of the Primitive Church, discover that in many things we have erred in our endeavour to fulfil the Divine will, and we earnestly desire now to reform the system of our Divine Church ; we have been enlightened to understand the will of the Almighty more clearly ; we have hitherto complained of Protestantism as a schism, but have forgotten that our human mistakes, and abuse of the unalterable truth, have caused the separation, and for which separation there would have been no excuse on the part of the Protestants, had we not *first* sinned in introducing a false element into the Church, by which error crept in. Christianity should be one thing,—the simple truth as Christ taught, and as little diversity in outward forms of public worship as possible ; every nation, in having its own church, should follow the one universal rule established, so that each national church could meet, and unite in doctrine and in worship. It has been found that Protestantism is no more all perfect than Catholicism, proving that we have not yet decided upon the *pure middle* path, and this greater perfection can only be realized in the true reform of the Roman Catholic system in returning to the practice of the Primitive religion. Therefore it is required that each side of the Christian Church should be magnanimous, in sinking *self-interest* and all favourite ideas and opinions: to be reasonable and ready to join hands for the reunion of Christendom. We, the governing powers of the Holy Roman Church, resolve to return to the purity of the Primitive Church as ordained by Christ Himself when upon earth, at the same time not omitting to give Him the outward honour due to Him in our public services, for in this point the Protestants do err in an extreme.

We will maintain our universal Head, and we will work disinterestedly for each soul and member of our body, endeavouring to carry out God's will in *its integrity;* and after this purification takes place, if any separate from the Reformed Church, the sin will be upon his own head; we leave him in the hands of God to receive his just correction. What we *first* propose to do, is to make religion *voluntary*, and *disinterested;* we issue it by *invitation*, to promulgate the word of God, and to act upon it in its practical simplicity, avoiding abstruse knowledge, which is too wonderful for us as mortals to attain unto—we will simply adhere to what is practicable and instructive. In public worship, we will retain the service of the

C

Holy Mass (without the belief of Transubstantiation, and other services, as Benediction, and all else that is beneficial for praise and adoration to the Lord of Hosts. Private devotion and meditation being a distinct part of our Christian life. In public worship the worshippers must surround a symbolical throne of Grace in the shape of an imposing altar, formed in the purest taste—the congregation losing sight of the world, during the celebration of Mass, each person, casting himself down as in the presence of the Holy Trinity, would adore his Lord and Master, with his whole heart, mind, and spirit. (In the Protestant churches few understand what true public worship is.) The Scriptures should be read in the language of the country, and reverently, and the finest hymns sung. Still speaking as the Head of the Church, I would again proclaim that *compulsory* auricular confession should forthwith be abolished as an obnoxious invention of man, and opposed to God's will, as is also the *enforced celibacy of the priests.* God would have each soul come directly to the SAVIOUR to be cleansed, and the priest's duty is to urge each one to confess his sins to the Saviour, and to learn with the aid of the Holy Spirit to purify his life, and to *watch* and *pray* that he may be kept in the right way. I would discourage the UNDUE worship of the Blessed Virgin, or individual saints, such as have been canonized by man ; honour them as Christ's friends, and let the whole army of Saints, Prophets, and Martyrs, be religiously remembered in a general way, and the Blessed Virgin honoured in a hearty spirit, after the manner her dear Son has appointed, during public service, every voice should proclaim aloud, 'Hail, Mary, full of grace as we give thee due praise, so also do thou pray for us, if thou hast the power, and may the souls of the dear departed sleep in peace according to Thy will, O God.' I, as the head of the Church, forbid any political motion or action to govern or influence religion. We will continue to exercise our charities to the poor, the afflicted, the sick, or the needy, under the best and purest organization ; and we invite the laity as a bounden duty to assist us according to the means of each one, either with money or personal help. All our convents and religious houses shall be free, any person to enter *voluntarily*, and to leave as they choose. —So far, I have supposed myself as speaking as the Head of the Church; I now speak for myself, and say such suggestions as the above are sufficient for your Holiness to act upon, and if acted upon would *draw* all men to be united to Christianity; there would then be but one Universal Christian Church. 'Ultra-montane' and 'Infallibility' are un-Christian names, and bring forth un-Christian principles, wrought of men, and not of God ; your Holiness must have seen already the disastrous effect of such dogmas. It was a human mistake, to dictate such impossible terms to your followers, the greater number of whom cannot believe a falsehood, and therefore remain in the Church with an insincere heart, and under bondage. Do not fear to put an end to this mistake, and clear the atmosphere of the Universal Church, that every human soul may enter into its legitimate home upon earth, and by the increase of its inmates, the numerous sects of Protestants may come to an end.

In closing my necessarily short petition, I must remind your Holiness that you and your colleagues have believed, and taught as a *fact*, the reputed vision of Mary Alacocq at Paray-le-Monial. will you believe me also, when I declare to you most solemnly that I have had a vision, and it occurred at three several times — two nights in succession at Windsor in the month of February 1872, and the third time in the same month upon the following year (viz. February, 1873)? On the occasion of the first two visions, I was sleeping in the house of the Queen of England's family nurse at Windsor, and the last time also at Windsor, but not in the same house. The difference between the Paray-le-Monial vision and of mine is this, the former was produced by an unnatural state of mind and body, whilst *awake;* the latter was simply and vividly shown to me in my sleep, without any *clue* to such a vision passing through my mind prior to the event, nor was I in an unhealthy state mentally or physically. I first saw the heavens open, and like a beautiful picture the clouds were tinted with a bright red colour, a large red cross was visible, and above it a circle representing the throne of Grace, in the which stood our Blessed Saviour surrounded by His friends, and smiling sweetly upon me. I repeated the Lord's Prayer, and He said, 'Teach the Church,' and then the open clouds closed up. I awoke with a calm, happy feeling, ideally seeing the same picture I had seen in my sleep; the next night, the vision was repeated, and not again until the following year, when the vision was slightly changed. Instead of the colouring being *red*, it was of a bright *golden* hue, and this time the heavens opened with something like a rocket firework, bursting quietly, leaving its spray to fall to the earth. Again I was told to teach the Church, when the heavens closed immediately, and I awoke, saying, ' I am so sorry it did not last longer, it was so beautiful.'

Now, your Holiness, I have spoken as from Heaven, for no mortal is allowed more than a passing glimpse of the invisible world ; and very wisely is it so ordained, for we could not at present endure the bright glory and excellence which is to come. In communicating my vision to you, *my responsibility* ceases ; *yours*, and that of the Primitive Church, remains. Almighty God, through His Son, desires you to cleanse and purify His earthly Church, to make it inwardly and outwardly as it was in the beginning, without the ugly excrescences which have since been introduced, and grown up, by man's invention. The human element in the Church is *selfish*, looking either for worldly ambition or supposed spiritual advantages, when every motive and movement in religion should be carried out in Christ's spirit, in a tone at once reasonable, and yet perfectly disinterested. If this pure spirit, this pure motive were more studied, man's general character would improve by the infection of good example ; then all who voluntarily divided from the Church of Christ would be guilty of a moral and wilful sin, without a shadow of excuse for their separation. Unity is strength, and in the reform and purification of the Holy Catholic Church, you would behold the grand union of Christendom,

which Christ our Head, at this moment, desires. May
God bless your Holiness, and all around you ; and may
the Holy Spirit prompt you to obey the Divine command, so that you may be spared a sorrowful reproof
hereafter

I remain in Christ,

AN ENGLISHWOMAN

*Written at Nice,
February, 1874.*

'What our Christianity is, and what it should
be,' or an Appendix to the Pamphlet called
'An Address to the Rev. Père Hyacinthe,
by an English Lady.'

The preceding words conclude a pamphlet written more
than a year ago, when my heart was stirred by the convic-
tion that perfect Christianity in all its bearings was to be
found only in the true balance of the two extremes—
between Ultramontanism on the one side and ultra-Protestantism on the other ; and although the little work has not
been advertised or widely circulated, yet by whomsoever it
has been read, or by whichever party, it has been so highly
commended for its simple truths and unbiassed spirit, that I
am encouraged to try my best efforts to more fully develope
what remains to be said upon the practical faults of our
Christianity of to-day, and the true remedies for bringing
about something like order out of the chaos into which our
soul-comforting, grand religion has, alas ! been degraded by
the human mistakes, the human sufficiency, of the present
times. To every thoughtful mind, or even to the super-
ficial observer, there is an instinctive consciousness that
the spiritual life is undergoing a transformation. Let us,
therefore, consider what are the chief causes, and what are to
be the results, of this change. One of the chief causes is, that
the material world is altered. Formerly, every particle of

life was brought into use more slowly: the civilised countries were not so full of human beings struggling for an
improved social position—each mind worked naturally and
without undue effort; even the greatest minds and the
greatest genius arrived at perfection more slowly, more
steadily—giving forth to the world enduring, perfect truths,
upon which the same order of mind in the present day
cannot improve in principle, although it may give a new
form, a more brilliant development and effect, to the
original truths and conceptions. It is like putting an em-
bellished case or outer crust to a kernel—the former will
attract by its outward beauty, and look more important, but
the latter is the *gem* containing the true worth—the unalterable first truth, as it has been handed down from the
Divine origin, to take up its place in the human intellect
of the first living genius—the first authors of all sublime
ideas. As we all know, the law of human progress has
stretched marvellously and rapidly throughout the last
century. Every one is conscious of the steam-force, the
propelling power which gives the impetus, and urges us
on, whether we will or no. To this state of things is found
in one way an advantage, in another a disadvantage,
proving that although man may continue to change the
manner of invention, that after all there is a *limit* to his
cleverness; for whenever he attempts to overstep the
boundary, the Almighty, the only Creator, immediately
checks His child, and brings him down to his proper level.
Some people murmur and complain that times are not
so good as they used to be; many more, however, are
enriched with this world's goods, and enjoy them to their
heart's content; yet even they, together with those who
complain, are never fully satisfied, nor, as a rule, are their
characters improved by their abundance. When man

rests his happiness entirely upon the material world, he is sure some day to be disappointed, because he wearies of every novelty after he has tried it. He at length discovers that he has a *soul*, and that this soul wants *food*. It cannot be fed here below—it yearns for food of a *higher* order. His religion must supply this want. And, therefore, the only tolerable and true happiness for mortal man is, of himself, and according to his circumstances, to balance the material with the spiritual. The spiritual life must be the foundation, the substratum, of the outer and practical life; because then, when the soul is sad with its earthly struggles, it can with confidence look *above*, and with child-like faith be *sure* that all will be well in the end, if only he feeds on the right food and trusts implicitly in the Divine power. Doubtless, in less restless times, and with less religious agitation, man, on the whole, was happier in his simple, unquestioned faith; but the state of society and the human mind having become more unsettled and inquiring, as a consequence so also has the spiritual atmosphere. Here, then, rests the *cause* of the transformation—in that the material and secular world has entered into another phase of existence, socially and morally changing its outside crust or fashion. Before noticing the result, let us bear in mind, that however much our Christian society may be agitated, its sure foundation, Christ Jesus, with His doctrines, are *unchangeable*—they are once and for ever the same. What we see around us is simply this: that since the foundation of the temporal Church upon the spiritual, man, through his infirmities, has taken upon himself to deform his religion, and to use it for interested purposes—man, in the form of the *head* of the original Church, with its appointed priests, has disobeyed Christ's intentions, and misled his fellow-man in many points of the otherwise excellent Church system. Hence the revolt of its subjects—hence the word 'Protestant' instead of 'Catholic' Christian! Had the popes and their priests held and taught the faith in its integrity, we never should have witnessed such a complex state of things as exists in the present day. Well may the heathen and the Jew ask, What is your Christianity, and in what is it better than our own faith? Let us witness the *daily practice* of your higher Christian principles, instead of the mere profession of them. Without doubt, there is but one true Christian Church upon earth—the representation and counterpart of the spiritual Church above ; and one corresponds with the other in faith, doctrine, and action. The Divine Essence is perpetually descending upon the institution, and upon such of its members who are worthy ; whilst at the same time, all that is Divine in the human ascends from the altar and symbolical throne below to the real heavenly throne above. This one true Church, as originally constructed by Christ, *is the only deposit of faith,* from whence all other Christian denominations derive their one-sided particle of Divine food. To these will be given according to the purity of their heart's motive, whilst they will hereafter regret they did not enjoy *to the full,* Christ's gifts and consolations here below. How far better would it be, then, if every Christian were united in one body, one baptism, one Lord, one faith ; and how grievous to find, in all days, the head of the Church and his coadjutors have been the cause of its anarchy and discord, and more so to find that at this moment (spite the personal goodness of him who is now in office) they obstinately refuse to reform the mistakes of their rule, which are at once an offence to Christ and Christ's people. In the first days of Christianity the construction of the holy Church was altogether pure and divine, and this purity and divinity still exist in the Roman Catholic Church, especially in the preservation of the public service of the Mass, being the true form from which Protestants have diverged. Hence the reason why so many people are tempted to join this Church. Better, say they, to take some human error in the original institution, than to be fed upon the diluted nourishment in the Protestant establishment, where still we find imperfection—where we lose so much consolation from the sins of omission. Many there are also who, like myself, cannot conscientiously or formally join the Church of Rome as she now exists, but who have to content themselves by being a Christian *outside* it, attending the beautiful services, and receiving such comfort as is offered in them. Once take away the *forcing* system as illegitimately used in the Romish Church, and, as by a *miracle*, the whole spiritual Christian Church would be changed—numbers would gladly flock in, as one fold under one Shepherd, because then the law of Christ would have effect, and universal, disinterested love would pervade the system—the head of the Church, with his priests, would issue Christ's commands by invitation. 'Come unto Him' would be the constant exhortation, and all who loved Jesus and their own souls would come and prostrate themselves before the Divine Master, to do Him outward and inward honour in the midst of the assembly. The officers of the Church are right in wishing to guard Christ's religion—in being firm over the authority entrusted to them—only that the authority should be exercised *morally*: the doors should be thrown open wide—the entrance *free*. This is Christ's desire; but unfortunately His officers with the keys act not after this manner. The man asserts himself more than he is bound to—he makes human laws to coerce his fellow-man. The question for them and for us to put to ourselves in these days is, not what does man teach, but what does *Christ* teach? What does *He* wish us to do? He has said, I appoint a *head* to my temporal Church, to teach as I taught, that by the power of the Holy Ghost both he and the priests may guide, and remind their fellow-men of the same two grand truths of Christianity (and we all need the constant repetition)—'Do thy duty to God and thy duty to man.' Our appointed teachers err in commanding their followers to come *first* to them, saying, Honour me, and I will transmit the honour to Christ. I whom you see am *infallible*. Believe on me, and then you will believe on Christ. Rather should he say, I, the head of the Church, wish you to see in me one who holds the responsible office of Christ's vicar on earth. I and my coadjutors are your spiritual teachers, to direct you according to Christ's law of love, that we may all be in fellowship with Him. Our unity is our strength. Our public services, at which we officiate, are instituted for our souls' comfort and consolation. When you are perplexed or discouraged with your daily trials, come to your natural home here below; and if you *volunteer* confession, we will hear and aid you, but we do not enforce it. Here, in the Church, you will find a heaven upon earth; the ideal part of your nature will be soothed by the sympathy of the Divine element—by the help of music, a legitimate altar, where, as mortal, you may, through the symbol, realise the throne of grace. You will see the image of your Saviour, His blessed mother, and other friends of our Lord. Your soul can commune with them; the *Dove* too will be there—the symbol of the Holy Spirit—to overshadow you, and each part of the Divinity will be united to the Holy Father through the man Christ Jesus. The blessed gift of God's dear Son will carry the mortal to immortality—the crucified

Saviour is the grand link which has been given us to unite earth to heaven, man to his Creator, and in the end to cast us in safety on the ground of an eternal world of happiness. Christ never told His apostles to *enforce* any-thing. I show you the happiness offered you; come and drink when you are thirsty—watch and pray—then let the action of your daily life accord with the earnestness and sublimity of your prayers. Come to the descendants of the apostles if you wish, and we will help you, as our Master has commanded us to help you. Should you wish to make confession of your sins or difficulties—if it be any consola-tion to you to speak to your fellow-man, who in his office is authorised to hear you—we will, with the grace of God bestowed on us, guide you to Him who is always ready to heal the broken-hearted, to forgive the sins of those who *repent*. In return, the laity are bound by the same authority to supply their priests with material food and raiment. As regards the celibacy of the priests, Christ made it optional. As St. Paul declares, it is better, if any have the greater strength, to serve his Lord *alone*. But such are the few. For the larger number, who would live naturally and honourably, marriage is the safer course; and in this state the priest may set forth a pattern of holy family life, for we should ever remember, that in the state of matrimony a man or woman may either exceed the law or obey it in moderation. One may be exceedingly pure in this state or just the reverse. It is in the cultivation of *moderation* that a man or woman can best obey the Creator. The enforced celibacy of the priests too often leads to sin; and it is too horrible to suppose that a priest or his work can be blessed if he live in open or concealed sin, for without pure morality where is the holiness without which none can see God? 'To the pure, all things are pure;' and to a right-minded man or woman the ordinance of marriage is *pure*, because sanctified by Christ. Therefore it should ever be a *religious* ceremony, performed in a church, and not a mere civil compact. Many persons have blamed Père Hyacinthe for marrying after having made the vow of chastity. I honour him for breaking the unnatural, enforced vow. Better to give the world the holy example that marriage is honourable—that he prefers to obey *God's law* rather than that of man, under the influence of which he might, like too many of his brethren, have done worse, and sinned. Let every soul strive to obey God *first;* to be sure that his conscience is right with the Divine law. Oh! when will this grand Catholic Church be purified? All honour to Père Hyacinthe, Dr. Döllinger, and their followers, who have had the moral courage to break through the human trammels, and stand apart, *still the true Catholic*, until Christ shall change the offences which have defiled His omnipotent institution! Cleanse and purify the Church, and we shall all be one in Christ Jesus. Anything like party spirit or political motive in religion should be abolished, as contention stirs up anger; and sweet, smiling charity, the foundation of Christianity, and the very bond of peace, is concealed, or altogether wanting in the soul, where a fiery party spirit reigns supreme. Let us all be liberal Catholics, and there will no longer be any excuse for divisions in Christianity. There may yet be some who will still set up a form of worship of their own, but they will be in the minority, and without excuse. We want no *novelties* in religion as in secular or material things. Each nation can still have its own Church, whilst each will be a branch of the one foundation. The public services and organisation of church-work should be the same all over the world—the mass, the benediction service, and other prayers, should be uni-

versally established. Speaking of *novelties*, I would here
refer to Messrs. Moody and Sankey's so-called mission.
With all due respect to these well-meaning gentlemen, I
cannot, as one of Christ's followers, approve of laymen
taking upon themselves to teach and preach the Gospel,
because it is contrary to our Lord's will, who would have
duly appointed ministers for that purpose. Privately and
en famille we may help each other in practising our religion, and give a kind word in season to those living
without God in the world; but for laymen to put themselves in the position of appointed ministers is not becoming, and anything like revivalism or undue excitement
upon religious questions is productive of more harm than
good. In the first place, it degrades the mystery and
solemn reverence which belongs to holy things. Anything
like claptrap for catching men's souls is objectionable either
in Catholic or Protestant. Some persons argue in favour
of revivalism outside the Church, saying the seed may be
sown and bring forth some fruit, where otherwise it would
never have reached. Granting that may be so, no one has
any right to use other means for preaching the Gospel than
the one already appointed; and for some souls that are thus
awakened, a good many others turn into dangerous fanatics;
and religion is not intended to drive men mad, but to
save them from madness. I have often been surprised to
notice how even the educated, the highest in social position,
will run after and patronise a Spurgeon, or a Moody and
Sankey; go into an opera-box to listen to a discourse from
the stage as if we had hitherto learned nothing of Christianity, nor had any *consecrated churches* wherein to hold our
solemn services of prayer and praise to the Most High.
The truth is, the *novelty* pleases; it becomes one of the
fashions of the day, and where one leads many follow. The

excitement of the novelty at length wears out, and leaves but little enduring fruit behind. To my mind it *degrades religion*. Better far if we encouraged and supported a large number of orthodox clergy and took some trouble to ensure that the poor, the unhappy, and the sinful, were tended by them. Another thing I have noticed with these new teachers is, that they find their strength and popularity in the use of the very same means practised by the Roman Catholics. What is it that has power over the soul of man, and excites a warmer devotion in worshipping his Creator? Is it not the assembling of ourselves together for His praise, to make known our requests to Him in prayer? is not the chief help found to be in the *best music*, in the preacher being earnest in speaking of our crucified Saviour and His divine love in dying for sinful man? I am told that Messr. Moody and Sankey not only use these powerful aids to convert others, but that they also practise the method employed at the Brompton Oratory—that of requesting members of the congregation to come forward and recommend particular cases for prayer—for instance, the conversion of one or more members of a family. Others are invited to speak of their own spiritual state in such a manner as proves the system to be tantamount to private confession. In stating a paradox, may we not then say how little novelty there is after all in our Christian religion, and how much better it would be to follow the one appointed method, without exaggeration or undue excitement? I am told, again, that unity in religion is impossible, owing to the diversity of men's minds—that the form of worship that suits one does not suit another. This also is a mistake. In a secular or political movement men are allowed to exercise and enjoy their own opinions, their varied strain of thought, but in Christianity its founder did not institute more than *one faith*, one form of worship, one doctrine, to which every variety of mind was to submit. Each of the apostles had a different character, a different order of mind; yet still they were not at variance in their mode of worship or preaching. What Christ instituted they taught. Every variety of mind was blended in His teaching, and brought into submission to His authority, whilst in their every-day social life they enjoyed the sober liberty of acting according to their own motives and their own wishes. Here, then, we have an authority for a practical unity in our religion. As there are many parts to be weighed in forming the whole of our Christian faith, it must be remembered, that so long as we remain upon earth we can never rid ourselves of the responsibility of duty, first towards God, and then to our neighbour. Nor can the intelligence always be absorbed in the supernatural and the world to come. As mortals we have to *work here*, and to bring our thoughts down to its work. The brain at intervals requires legitimate relaxation. Merriment and amusement are good pastimes, and there is a time for such indulgence. We should strive to give a healthy tendency to our amusements. For some part of the day we may laugh with child-like mirth—making joy out of small things —at the same time helping the children to their games. And to enable us thus daily to rejoice in the Lord, we must continually go for a fresh supply of food to the *Christian altars* in the church—to converse with our Saviour, our best and unchangeable Friend. Earthly friends may change and leave us, but Christ is ever to be found upon the altar dedicated to His honour, where we may look at His image and speak to Him as if he were visible; where we may realise that He is near to our hearts and we to His. Here we may ask the Dove to hover o'er and comfort us—then when sorrow or death overtake us, we shall not be alarmed. We shall behold the beautiful vision of the other world through the curtain that now divides it from us ; we shall smile as we receive the smile of the angels, who may be the spirits of our own dear departed, who are ready to welcome us where there will be no more mystery, no more pain or sorrow. Although so far I have principally alluded to the Roman Catholic Church as the one true Church, spite its human errors and need of reform, I must not omit to mention the Eastern, or Russian Church, as a branch of the same, for, except in not acknowledging the Pope as its head, it is in form of worship, belief, and doctrine, very similar. Indeed to my mind there is even more sublimity in its services and its vocal music, whilst in the prostration of the body of its worshippers we see an Oriental form. I think I am right in stating that auricular confession is not *enforced*, but advocated, and the priests are permitted to marry one wife. With these advantages over the Roman Church, there would be no difficulty in bringing it into union with a reformed Christianity, after the pattern of the Primitive Church ; nor do I suppose that our Anglican, American, or various other branches of Episcopalians, would hesitate to follow and fall in, to fill up the ranks round the one chosen head and representative of the Reformed Church. Our Anglican, and more cold Protestant ideas would have to warm up to meet the warmth of the outer devotion of our Eastern Christian brethren, whilst the heart of an Englishman would be still as full of love to his Redeemer if he moved his body in reverence, or crossed himself before the Lord, to give him the outward proof of his inward spirit. With the reform made by the Pope, or head of the Church, and the abolition of his temporal power (save the possession of the Vatican, St. Peter's, and other sacred buildings), none could justly dispute his authority to rule Christendom by the strength of the Holy Spirit, by the free love of Christ. In order to effect this great perfection, each party must be ready to give up some pet idea, each member must sink self to please our Great Master. When men will consent to accomplish this grand design, then will Heaven smile more gladly upon our world of self-torment and misgovernment; then will the crooked ways be made straight, then shall we realise what it is to love our brethren, and to be real Christians after God's own heart. I would once more emphatically impress upon all Protestants that the MASS is the true and most perfect form of public worship. The Communion Service in the Church of England holds the same idea without the belief in transubstantiation; yet why this discussion about the real presence in the bread and wine? Whether it is corporal or spiritual, it is enough to know and believe that Christ has chosen to give Himself in this form, and that therefore we may not trifle with, or partake lightly of His divine essence and purity, which is the only real food for our souls on earth. There is no Christianity without *love;* if we feel this love in our hearts for our Redeemer we shall be glad, and not hesitate to partake of Him, and in the celebration of the Mass we shall realise His one sacrifice once made for us; we shall use the beautiful prayers for the service, and participate in the passion of our Lord; and as the bell sounds for the most *solemn moment,* we shall bow down before Him in reverent silence, and contemplate the Saviour crucified for us. In the Scotch Presbyterian Church they have diluted Christ's institution still further by administering it but twice a-year! How many souls must *die* in the long interval without partaking of the food that has been given for our souls' nourishment! Some people again object to what is called too much sentiment in religion, and complain of an over-abundance of it amongst the party called 'Ritualists.' Without any reference to this maybe well-intentioned, but misplaced community in the Church of England, I would remind the former objectors that there is a true and a false sentiment; that of real sentiment there cannot be too much in the worship of our Creator and our Redeemer, for religion is sentiment, and 'God is love.' It is generally overlooked that our Christianity is composed of many parts, and that each part should be balanced. The reason there are so many sects and divisions is, because many persons ignorantly interpret one part of Scripture, or one verse, and form their notions of religion upon it; this fault has, on the one hand, given rise to the mistake of the Catholics in forbidding their members the free use of the Bible.

With regard to our Jewish brethren, I often think we are wanting in gratitude to them for all the ancient learning they have handed down to us, and that the persecution to which they have been subjected is a blot and stain upon the Christian name. It has been a terrible mistake of false zeal, and were it only that our dear Lord in His humanity was a Jew, we should for His sake have respected the ancient people, and sought to reconcile them by the exercise of a more Christian spirit. Happily, in these days they stand in a better social position all over the world, and still more happily with the change they are beginning to view our crucified Redeemer in a less prejudiced light; their blind obstinacy is giving way to a glimmer of light, which, with the help of the Holy Spirit, will shine more, and more near and nearer to the perfect day, when all nations and all peoples shall be reconciled in the Alpha and Omega, the brightest star in heaven, around which gem every earthly soul shall be lighted up, immortalised, to add its brightness to the one transcendant glory. The Jewish faith was ordained of God, and preceded our own. Christianity was based upon it; Christ came not to do away with the ancient law, but to re-model and make the old religion more perfect. And now let me add, if we desire a purer practical state of Christianity, it is necessary, that, individually and collectively, we earnestly strive for a greater degree of moral excellence, as being the great point of higher perfection : that part of our religion which proves it to be *superior* to any other. Christians have become very *lax* in their morality, so that they have fallen even lower than the heathen, who do not recognise the moral law. It is a terrible fact and disgrace to the Christian profession, and whilst exercising the greatest pity towards such who fall by chance and unfavourable circumstances, and to all who are penitent : to the habitual and unscrupulous sinner a severe punishment and reproof should be offered, for no sin can equal his in blackness and Satanic character. He is an object too loathsome to contemplate, and alas ! he dwells in every nation. But perhaps in Paris, a greater license is given to the open profligate ; a man in the highest society there will be thought none the less of for his habitual immorality, he is called a '*bon garçon*' whilst he is cruelly ruining the naturally pure in heart. It is to be hoped the French nation will learn to take a more serious view of this great fault, to realise the awful *sin* of trifling with God in the open disobedience of His moral law ; to *sin wilfully*, and then go to church to pray without repentance to the God whom they have offended, is a mockery ; and may it not be the sin against the Holy Ghost ? It is because my heart is warm towards the French people that I speak a warning word, and entreat them to do their utmost to lift themselves from this moral degradation, the indulgence in which has already injured their pleasant character and lovely country. They also set a bad example to sober-minded England, and other nations, who are ever fascinated by Parisian manners and fashions.

Paris, and France as a nation, are necessary to the whole world, let her then pride herself upon showing a better example, and a purer moral atmosphere. Her people need be none the less fascinating and agreeable in a social point; there is a way of being natural in a pleasant manner, in being gay and fascinating, which is quite consistent with a religious and pure mind. Let the French people be valued for their *goodness* as well as for their pleasantness. Let them advocate *marriage* with pure affection, in the place of cold worldly alliances, or illicit connexion. Believe me! everything that is pure, good, and natural, will conquer in the end and bring eternal bliss; whilst that which is false will fade away, and die in everlasting sadness. I was never on the Continent till two years ago, and now I love France, and can from the heart (without any political motive or party spirit) sing with the people, ' Sauvez, sauvez la France au nom du Sacré Cœur!' for this cause would I have her purified from her faults. By-the-by, this dévotion of the Sacred Heart of Jesus, which has now been particularly adapted by the Church to the French nation, is a very beautiful idea; may we all cultivate such pure virtues, as to be more worthy to enter into the sacred heart of Jesus, and that He may be able to enter into our hearts. Thus may the love of God, which passeth all understanding, keep our hearts and minds to everlasting life. Christianity teaches us to cultivate a cheerful spirit, under all conditions of life. Sorrows and trials *must come*. Our faith then teaches us that brave hearts and fortitude can make us endure the severest trial, and from personal experience I would exhort all my fellow-Christians never to shrink from, or be afraid of *intense suffering*, if it be necessary to pass through the boisterous wave, or to taste of the bitter cup of Gethsemane. If we lean upon the loving heart of Jesus, who first suffered for us, we shall rise up all the stronger, all the better for having united our sufferings with His. There is such a thing as 'rejoicing in suffering;' the sufferer for the moment will cast off his mortal coil, he may afterwards show a more cheerful countenance than before, and with a good conscience he will, with purified mirth, act as a social radiator to everyone around him.

Finally, I would allude to that most perplexing, and difficult question which has been so much mooted of late: namely, what relation has the Church with the State? or which has the prior authority, the Pope, the Queen, King, or Emperor? It seems to me that the same theory should apply to this, as to all other questions affecting the general welfare. As far as possible one power should balance the other; one should be reconciled to the other. The heads of nations have power and responsibility from heaven, to govern their kingdoms for the happiness and welfare of their people: and if the people revolt under a just government, the head of it has the right to use its power, and with a just and firm hand to put down rebellion and bring the agitators to reason or punishment. But if, on the other hand, the head of a government fail in his duty to his people, the people will rise against him and anarchy will prevail. When this is the case, or when any Christian nation forgets God, and sin abounds, then the head of the Church *has a right and power so to do*, in the name of Christ to remonstrate with the rebellious, to speak disinterestedly for Christ, by reminding the disobedient, that as Christians, they must change their conduct and serve their Master better. But this jurisdiction and power can only be exercised *morally*, and the moral power ought to be sufficient for all parties; indeed the Pope, not being divine, but divinely instituted in his office, has no undue right or influence; but his voice, as far as its line extends, should be respectfully listened to and heeded. It certainly is permitted by word of mouth, to correct the errors and sins of mankind: and if this be the true, just, and kindly voice it should be, and if nations and people would, with reverence for the divine authority, follow the good counsel, how often we should be spared the powerful judgments sent from Heaven, which, because we are disobedient to the gentle persuasions of His ministers in the Church, He Himself is compelled to come forth and reprove us with greater severity; to avoid so great a calamity why do not the Church and State separately walk side by side, one trying to harmonize with the other; the State partially supporting the Universal Church, or their own nation's part of it, with annual sums of money for the Church and its charitable services. The Church can do no more than reprove its rebellious subjects, it cannot *coerce*. She is, however, the seat of divinity upon earth, and should be respected and reverenced as such; and are we not too often disobedient children who because the Holy of Holies is out of sight, forget His invisible presence amongst us: and because we cannot see God we go astray; for this reason is it necessary for us to go to Christ and His ministers for instruction, to frequently attend the Holy Ordinances, to pay almost daily visits to His altars, to pray, to converse, and commune with our best Friend, and to ask for the Holy Spirit's direction. Protestants have erroneously been taught that altars, and Catholic Church decorations are superstitious appendages, but are they not simply used as *helps* to a higher faith? for if we come to analyze the meaning, we shall find how small an subtle is the difference between the two words superstition and faith. Does not the *Invisible* create a *mystery*, and does not the Protestant better realize the Unseen when he enters a Catholic Church? Is not his heart warmed with devotion, spite of his educational prejudices, when at length he looks up at the altars and pictures, and hears the music which reminds him of heaven? Unfortunately, very often the benefit of these holy aids is defeated and degraded by the sight of dolls dressed as virgins and saints in tawdry tinsel, and arranged in the worst possible taste. Every church decoration should portray the presence of the holy people and their associations, and be in the best possible taste; herein the Russian Church excels. *Apropos* of paintings and sculpture in churches, let me disabuse the minds of those who are prejudiced against them and regard those who kneel before an image as guilty of idolatry, by asking them to think quietly for a moment, and ask themselves what God intended us to understand by idolatry. When He forbade us to make graven images or to worship them, He was speaking to the heathen who worshipped *false gods*, or to those who make idols of their fellow-creatures? Our Saviour has never forbidden us to worship Him through the sight of His image, short as it may fall of the reality. Our Lord, His mother, the apostles, and all the good people who are absent from us, were men and women, and their holy features and spiritualised countenances, their martyrdom and their faith, have given sublime subjects for the painter and the sculptor, and our mortal nature becomes refined by the sight of them, when, through these images, we can better realize the unseen figures. How many a poor person in England might be kept from the public-house if they had Catholic churches to enter! What an exalted effect it would have upon the soul and mind of

E

such an one; for I always think the poor and wretched in our own country suffer more than do the same class abroad. Climate has a great effect upon the spirits. Where the sun shines there is naturally a greater disposition to cheerfulness; and the physical wants of a people under such circumstances are not so great; the air partly feeds them, and animal food suffices in a smaller quantity. I remember when I returned from India, my heart was excessively pained by the sight of the poor in London, with the rich equipages passing them by, as if the occupants had nothing in common with their poorer fellow-creatures. In India (except in the periodical times of famine), the poor can bask in the sun, require little clothing, and a small portion of cheap food. What a contrast exists between the state of the poor in one country and the other! The rich people in England have to see that their poor, as well as the working classes, have fitting dwelling-houses, since the climate demands home life. There should be large buildings fitted up for innocent amusements; every consideration and help should be given to this class of people, to improve their moral and religious lives. A great deal has already been done, and some of our rich are very charitable, but we need a better organization for our charities, whether carried out on a small or a large scale; and above all, a less patronizing spirit in giving to those who are less fortunate than ourselves.

In closing my few general remarks, upon the reform of our religious and moral state of Christianity. I would impress upon my readers that, after pointing out the way and the means to be used for this general improvement. I am quite sensible of the existing difficulties towards this great perfection. But having had a *vision*. and a command from heaven, as clear as could be given to mortal between sleeping and waking, I could not resist the inspiration to make known the will of God, as it appears to my mind. My mission is now at an end. I have addressed Père Hyacinthe at Geneva, and the Pope at Rome; the latter address is now published, and I have, in these general remarks made known the purport of my mission to the public. I hope my earnest convictions simply given, may be kindly received, and that the *truth*, however difficult in execution, may be carried out individually and collectively. The *result* of course is with a Higher Power, who wishes us to help Him with one consent here below.

May our Reformed Christianity after the pattern of the primitive Catholic Church convert the unbeliever. May it reconcile the Jew and the Christian, the Heathen and the Christian, the Ultramontane and the ultra-Protestant, the ordinary Protestant with the Catholic. May all be united under the one spiritual Head of Christ, and call themselves Catholic Christians, and may we respect and acknowledge the authority of the divinely appointed temporal head the Pope or Patriarch.

Let the Pope make the few necessary reforms, and then will be an end to the unchristian collisions between one and the other party ; and now, with every good wish for each of my kind readers, I cannot do better than close my address with my private motto,—'Spero Meliora.'

E. LAIRD.

Paris, June, 1875.

LONDON.
Printed by JOHN STRANGEWAYS, Castle Street, Leicester Square.

www.ingramcontent.com/pod-product-compliance
Lightning Source LLC
Chambersburg PA
CBHW081524040426

42447CB00013B/3329